RUSSIA-UKRAINE WAR:

2022 Russian Invasion in Ukraine

Chronicles – Part I

By Uliana Gabruk

Contents

Introduction

It's the 4th day of the war in Ukraine and I don't have many ideas, how to help my family and friends. I sent money to support our army, I repost everything in Instagram to show the world what's going on, go to meetings in the center of London, I read Ukrainian news every hour, possibly even more often, text my friends and family constantly and keep worrying about them... But today I caught myself thinking maybe I can write a small book to share with everyone scope and pain of this war. Not a military operation as Russian say...A real war, I think it's already World War 3, cause so many countries are involved... Sure, my English is far from perfect native speaker's English, but I hope you'll understand me and what I wanted to share with you.

I see what's in news in English speaking resources and what's in Ukrainian. And as Ukrainians say "It's just a drop in the ocean" in comparison with what I read every half an hour... You need to know more to understand who are Ukrainians, what is this war about and how to help.

I really want to share with you guys my pain, pain of my family and my friends, pain of every Ukrainian woman whose husbands, dads, brothers are dying in this war...

I'm sorry for my not perfect English, honestly... The real reason for this book is that I want you (as a foreigner) to know more than just "Putin started the war" against Ukraine. I want you to realise the scale of this war, I want you as a foreigner to feel that you want to help Ukraine. If you have money - donate to the Ukrainian army, you have some warm clothes - find a place where you can go and share it, you know some refugees who've just moved to your city because of the war- come to them, talk to them, help them to socialize... if it's still a war - urge your government to support Ukraine with defence ammunition and impose economic restrictions on Russia. Maybe when I finish the book (I pray for this) this war will be finished, maybe not, but I really try to help as much as I can and I kindly ask you to help and really hope that this small book will motivate you to care about Ukraine. No one knows what waits us tomorrow, but it is important to remain a human under any circumstances.

All the Earnings from Sales of This Book Will be Sent to Support Ukraine in the War Against Russia.

Before The War Started

and

A Little Bit About Me

My name is Uliana. It's not like Juliana, like Julia. It's like Ooliana, but anyway, most people don't spell it right. I was born in 1993 and raised in Ukraine in Cherkassy (a small city in the very central part of Ukraine, 2 hours by car from Kyiv). Then I moved to Kyiv to study dentistry and was living in Kyiv almost for 8 years. I left dentistry for publishing to work remotely but have never tried to write my own book. This will be my first one.

So, I spent most of my life in Ukraine and moved to London a few years ago... Most of my friends here are Ukrainians, I love different nationalities, but often when people go abroad it's easier to find friends who are your countrymen. My mom sadly passed away from cancer almost 2 years ago and that was a time when I could move to the UK to my dad who's also from

Ukraine, from west part of it. I need to say that he's a best borshch (you know - this red soup whit cabbage, beetroot and meat) cooker in the world. So for many years I was living a simple Ukrainian life then I moved to London. I still have a big Ukrainian part of me and visited Ukraine really often. Honestly, I've never thought that the war was coming till February 22.

My name is Steve Compton. For the past eight years I have swapped the UK for life in Ukraine. I made the decision to move to Kyiv in 2014 to work as an English teacher. I found a school and signed the contract in December 2013, 2 weeks later Maydan Revolution started and so there I was, January 1ˢᵗ, -20c degrees, no friends, not knowing any Ukrainian but was impressed to witness how proud Ukrainians were preparing Molotov cocktails in the centre of Kyiv to overthrow the pro-Russian government of Ukraine at that time. Since then, I knew that Ukraine was the country for me. I have met thousands of smart, well-bred, determined and brave people who despite harsh lives still smile, aim for a better life for their families, themselves and for Ukraine. A pleasure to see. I have felt, like most foreigners, so welcome. When you have a Ukrainian friend – you have a friend for life. Thank you Ukraine…. Dyakuju!

Slava Ukraini! – Heroyam Slava!

First Fears

It was 22 of February when my cousin Maiia sent me a message *"Улісітас, у нас війна починається. Це триндець"*. That is in English "Uliana, the war is coming. That's f*cked up!" She told me that a lot of Russian forces are amassing near Ukraine's borders. Putin said like it could only be there for a few days before being withdrawn back to adjacent bases".

I was like - maybe it doesn't mean a real war, maybe they'll come back, but why near the borders so? Russia is so huge; doesn't he have other places in this country to have trainings? Maybe it's a kind of some political tricks of President Vladimir Putin that was trying to increase pressure for some purpose. But, really - Russia vs Ukraine? No way. Couldn't be truth…

And it was 02/22/2022 a palindrome date. You know a date when people make wishes and at 22:22 I wished a peaceful sky in Ukraine, as I had this feeling of something bad was coming…

Then next day was quiet and then BOOM!

First Day of the War

February 24, 2022

On the night of February 24, Russian President Vladimir Putin in a video message announced the beginning of a "special military operation" against Ukraine. Explosions erupted in a number of Ukrainian cities. The Verkhovna Rada imposed martial law in Ukraine. After that, Russian troops attacked from the east, north and south. Seemed like they attacked Ukraine from everywhere. People were shocked. How was it possible? It seemed like in some movie, not like in real life... not about Ukraine...

First hours of attack   *Results of bombings on the first day of the war*

Russians launched rocket and bomb attacked on airfields in Boryspil, Ozernoye, Chuguyev, Kramatorsk, Kulbabkin, as well as on military facilities of the Armed Forces of Ukraine in Kyiv, Kharkiv, Dnipro and other parts of Ukraine. As you can see on the map, all the parts of Ukraine were attacked. The aggressor inflicted artillery strikes on settlements along the border. The president said he would issue weapons to anyone with combat experience and want to defend the homeland. Mass evacuation of population to the west part of Ukraine started.

All the Ukraine was like: How? WHY? What happened?

Every Ukrainian had lots of emotions of fear, of despair, of not acceptance, and not understanding. And this was, and still is a pain of Ukraine.

Also, many people didn't know what to do. The questions they asked themselves were: "Is it safe in my place? How long will it be safe? Is it safer to go to west part of Ukraine? Or maybe to go to Europe?"

But basically, it wasn't safe anywhere in Ukraine… Maybe just on the borders with EU.

FIRST DAY OF THE WAR RESULTS:

The clashes were particularly fierce near Sumy and in Gostomel near Kyiv, where the Antonov flying enterprise is located. The Armed Forces were forced to launch an artillery strike at the airport, where the enemy landed.

According to preliminary data, Ukraine had lost 137 citizens, 10 of them officers. 316 people were injured.

"Russian warship go f*ck yourself".

The aggressor also used combat aircraft against border guards and UAF fighters on Zmiiny Island. There, shelling from ship weapons continued almost all day. And, very soon the phrase of the military of this island will be the motto of this war.

Russian troops tried to intimidate Ukrainian defenders on the island with demands to surrender, but they courageously defended and answered them in Russian *Русский военный* *корабль, иди на x*й ",* which means "Russian warship go f*ck yourself".

There were 13 soldiers of this island, they are heroes of 21st century. The occupiers fired at Zmiiny Island from barreled ship weapons, then they used combat aircraft. Later in the evening, the State Border Service reported that communication with the border guards on Zmiiny was lost, probably the island was captured by the enemy.

"Russian warship go f*ck yourself"

All the dead militaries were awarded the title "Heroes of Ukraine" posthumously. On February 28, the Ukrainian Navy announced that the Ukrainian military from Zmiyiny Island were alive and, according to them, were in Russian captivity.

Russian troops captured the Chernobyl Nuclear Power Plant. The condition of the former Chernobyl facilities and nuclear waste storage facilities was unknown.

Can you even imagine if Russia blows up a nuclear power plant? If you haven't seen the film about Chernobyl- watch it and you'll realise how dangerous it is. It will be a catastrophe of the whole world, not just Ukraine.

There were hundreds of strafings:

- In Konotop district a car came under fire, as a result of which a woman with a child was injured.
- In the Odessa region in the city of Podolsk HF 0173 bombing, 6 dead, 7 wounded, 19 missing.
- In the city of Mariupol, Donetsk region, one person was killed and two were injured in the shelling.

But maybe you've never heard about those places. Just the thing is that on the first day of the war Putin said that he wouldn't hurt civilians, only military installations. But it was a great lie, not the first one from Putler. Sorry, but I can't say Putin, cause he's probable the Hitler of 21st century. The person who decided that no-one could stop him. Just he didn't expect that Ukrainians are brave and they will protect their families and Zelensky "will not need a ride".

Also, even on the first day were known that sabotage groups were in Ukraine and they will put some marks on the roofs, on the roads, as well as sent fake news to create more fear and panic among the people. Some of them were sent here in December, they hired flats and now they started their work. Don't tell me they didn't know what they would do here... Even a priest from the Russian Orthodox Church put marks on building. Marks were targets where to bomb...

Also, on a day 1 Boris Johnson announced some sanctions against Russia, Biden also reacted. But those sanctions weren't enough for now to stop the war and couldn't react fast. Later, the sanctions would be more serious and from many more countries, but it was just the start of the war. A few days later, on 27 Feb, all of the EU closed Swift for Russia and they closed the sky for Russia. This sanction would be tangible\. A flight Moscow-Berlin would take so long as a flight Moscow-Peking. But actually, Russian people would not be able to get to Europe anyway.

Second Day of the War

February 25, 2022

Day 2 was really hard. When I woke up and saw all those pictures I couldn't speak for a moment, was just crying..

I was living for 8 years in a beautiful Kyiv city, capital of Ukraine… And now it is being destroyed. So hard to recognise places where from ruins... Imagine you live in some nice city and when you come back you don't recognize it? Cause it turns to ruins…It still seems like not real for me, please wake me up… I don't want to watch this movie further…. But okay, forget about me... Those people whose flats were there… Maybe they were at home? I know a family who can't go anywhere from Kyiv, because they have an old woman that can't be moved anywhere because of health problems…

I texted and called my family, friends if they were okay... But in fact, no-one was okay in this situation. Seemed to me like they tried to support me more than I supported them ...I thought and still have this feeling - "how strong and brave are these people".

My bf is from Kharkiv and on a second day Kharkiv was damaged a lot too... His parents lived not far from Kharkiv and lots of our friends live in that city. It turned into a very dangerous place. But no-one knew if it would be safer to go somewhere then. No guarantee that you wouldn't be bombed or that you would not be crushed by a tank... Russian militaries were there and they shot civilians....

One of the fiercest battles was being fought in Kyiv region, as the occupiers were trying to break into the capital. This is their aim to conquer Kyiv, and then in their opinion other cities would surrender.

The Russian army was also shelling settlements in Kyiv region from Grad weapon. The Grad multiple launch rocket system (MLRS) had become the most common and extensively deployed in the world. In light of the launcher's ability to fire a whole salvo of 40 122mm rockets over an extensive region in less than 20 seconds, the name "Grad," which is Russian for "Grad," seemed appropriate.

In particular, an orphanage in Vorzel, Kyiv region, where 50 children were staying at the time. I don't know how, but they were not injured. I was completely shattered. Why were you shooting at kids? It's not their war...

The Russian occupiers fired at Kharkiv from the "Grad", one of the shells got stuck right in the middle of the road. The enemy attacked Sumy region, Chernihiv region, In the evening, the enemy broke through the defense of Kherson.

An important statement was made by NATO Secretary General Jens Stoltenberg. NATO has stepped up its defense plan and would provide Ukraine with air defense systems, that was really important, cause Russians attack a lot from the air, as they knew that it's Ukrainian weakness.

People were joking that this was how most popular cocktails in Ukraine looked like:

To protect Ukrainian cities and drive out the invaders, our military was enlisting the assistance of anybody willing to lend a hand. Recipes for "Molotov cocktails" (shown on the pictures before) IMHO, is known by every student in Ukraine now, also militaries asked to reports on enemy labels that should be destroyed as soon as they appear on the road.

With those cocktails people could even set fire to the tank and many brave people were stopping tanks with "Molotov cocktails". Some people tried to overtake the tank by car and threw this dangerous cocktail at them. No fear, just protecting their children from occupiers.

Also, interesting fact about these amazing Russian drink is that homeless people in Ukraine proposed to help collect bottles that's needed to prepare Molotov cocktails. Even they started to help!

Residents of high-rise condos were also being asked by police to restrict access to the rooftops of their properties since the roofs of residences might be marked for the occupants. Lots of them were found and eliminated by ordinary people.

Those marks first were just like painting, then they were with light, also they were using some mechanisms, that also were shown to people to be able to recognise and eliminate if found.

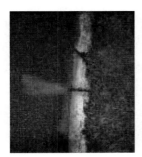  

But Ukrainians have a good sense of humour and they created this masterpiece:

I totally agree with it.

Also, some positive fact is: In Obolon (Kyiv), local Gopniks (slang term for chavs, street robbers) seized armored personnel carriers from Russian soldiers. They waited for the Ukrainian military forces and calmly handed them over. I wonder, how the commander explained to Putin, how gopniks stole an armored personnel carrier from them.

Day 2 Losses of the Russian occupiers

In the Chernihiv region, 20 enemy tanks were destroyed, as well as another 10-15 units of equipment moving to Chernihiv. Ukrainian troops also destroyed a column of Russians moving toward central Kyiv. They used enthusiastic Ukrainian vehicles.

In one and a half days, the Ukrainian military killed 2,800 Russians who invaded our country. This is really a huge number honestly. Units of the Armed Forces destroyed about 600 units of enemy equipment: armored combat vehicles of various types, tanks, planes and helicopters.

Russia had not suffered such a large number of casualties during such hostilities during its existence in any of the armed conflicts it has started.

Losses of the Ukrainian Armed Forces and civilians

On February 25, the General Staff of the Armed Forces of Ukraine announced a Marine from Ternopil, Vi-taliy Skakun, who had sacrificed his life to carry out a combat mission. The military blew up a bridge in the Kherson region with him to stop a column of Russian tanks.He was just 25 years old guy.

There were civilian casualties during the shelling in Kyiv region. The Kyiv City State Administration reported four killed and more than 15 wounded. People were instructed to hide in underground or in cellars, or in bunkers if there are some of them not far.

In the evening, the town of Ivankiv was shelled from the "Grad", fires were recorded there, and the press service of the Ministry of Internal Affairs reported casualties among civilians.

The enemy broke through the defense of Kherson, a child died in Okhtyrka, Sumy region, who was wounded by Russian troops when they fired on a kindergarten. In the region, the occupiers also fired on a civilian car, killing one person and another one was in a hospital.

The shelling also takes place in the center of Kharkiv. During the two days of Russian shelling in the Kharkiv region, 11 people were killed, including four militaries, and another 82 were wounded (23 militaries). Two main aims of Putler were Kyiv and Kharkiv, so they suffer the most among all the other cities. The head of the regional state administration said that the Blood Center and the school were shelled, and that there were casualties among the civilian population.

Here is a map of places where Russian attacked Ukraine. As you can see -they are everywhere.

A huge migration of refugees started even on the first day, but on the second it was much bigger. My cousins also decided that it was very dangerous to stay in Kiev and they tried to go somewhere to the village in Zhytomyr region. In most petrol stations they could get no more than 20 litres of fuel. Also in Kiev, some credit and debit card limits were applied. Often people needed cash and huge queues to ATMs couldn't be avoided.

Good news were that Ukrainians took the first prisoners of Russia. All of them were saying that they were going to military trainings, not to war. I've seen most of them were young, like 17-25 years old. Ukraine organised a hot line for moms of such Russian prisoners. But while listening to how they talked to parents, I had different emotions - like anger cause they were killing my motherland, but sympathy, cause they were young and they were just following military instructions, they were not commanders…

Some of them voluntarily surrendered when understood that it was a lie and they entered with guns and weapons to the independent country. But this was valuable information for our people. Cause they realised that our enemies were afraid more than us, because we were on our land. We protected our country, but they just followed someone's decisions and were lied to. So from this moment it turned to our superpower. Civilians started to go out and stop tanks by standing in front of the tanks, that they were going to ordinary people without guns and it was their land, not Russian.

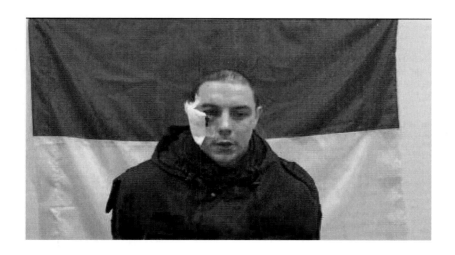

I'm really shocked how brave people could be without any weapon approaching tanks and simply asking not to go further and surrender. It's a kind of mental power and strong hope, that there is a human in a tank.

Also, good news that day for me was that one of my friends had a baby on that day. They of course had not expected him to be delivered in the basement of the hospital. It was really damp and cold, but it was safer. Children were born in underground stations; I can't imagine how their moms were feeling. Here are pictures how was it.

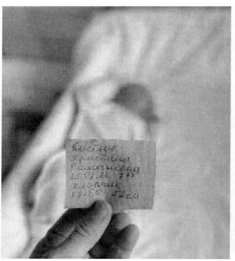

People all over the world started to go to their main squares to support Ukraine. Many capitals of the world and big cities today were marked by mass actions in support of Ukraine. Numerous rallies took place in Tallinn, Estonia, Budapest, Hungary, Bucharest, Romania, etc. A lot of cities started even on a day 1, but day 2 thousands of people gathered all over the world. Just look at these photos.

Third Day of the War

February 26, 2022

My close people:

My friend Galina has twins, 7 y.o girls, and they woke up the next morning because of a sound of shots or explosions, she couldn't describe clearly. When I texted her, she texted me back: "I don't know what's the date today, but it's 3rd day of the war…"

At night they were hiding in the basement of the house. Luckily, a few days ago they took some cash from ATMs and could buy some food in the market to feed children.

The mom of my friend, Jana, has 5 children. And what's important - 3 dogs, 5 cats and a horse in a village next to Kyiv. The first day they were in Kyiv, but it became to be very dangerous and they went to their village house, took one family there, and one more girl with a cat. But it turned out that the missiles that moving towards Kyiv were flying just over this village and also military base was very close, as well as an oil base near Vasylkiv that would be bombed so soon...But they couldn't leave the place, cause if they did - all the animals would be left for dead.

My friend Alexandra was in Kyiv and she decided to be a field nurse trying to help with everything to others.

My friend Alexandra who's from Dnipro she wanted to move to the West part of Ukraine, but her parents didn't want too. So she stayed in Dnipro and started to gather food for soldiers and those who need some food.

My cousins Maiia and Snezhana left Kyiv to the village in Zhytomyr region to family friends. She sent me some videos how empty markets were. And I've never seen something like that in Ukraine. Even when Covid started, they weren't so empty (just some lack of toilet paper).

Natalie another friend has a little son, she lived in Kyiv. Her brothers were soldiers. She took her son and her nephew to grandmas to the village in Ternopil. Usually it took 5 hours to get there, now it is more than 10...But she would go back and help in a hospital as she's a medic. A dentist, but dentists are doctors too, especially if it's a war.

One more of our friends Anton. He's from Kharkiv. And from the first day of the war he has started to hide in the basement with lots of people, just sometimes he went up to the flat to take some food. But, the number of sirens were incredible in Kharkiv and amount of destructions were and still are awful. He lived in the area that was fired on the most. Sometimes we didn't have connection with him and just praying that he's alive. Cause every time we watched the news that one new building there was being fired upon from "Grad" or tank or bomb caused a million emotions of fear for the person who is important to you...

In Kivsharivka (Kharkiv region) where the parents of my boyfriend lives have real problems with buying some food or medicine. Huge queues to small markets or bakeries, a lack of medicines... The reason was that the bridge was blown up by Ukrainian militaries so that Russian military equipment could not pass into the city. But the city is so small and all the products were brought in from Kharkiv. But for now, they had some products, but in the future no-one knows when the bridge would be restored. Also, when it was blown up, the gas pipe was damaged and it's winter time in Ukraine, it's really cold.

My friend Dan. We were having a video call and then it was interrupted by an explosion and he did not answer for about an hour...

People started saying that a message "How are you?" means now "I love you". And actually it was so, because you care if you ask...

What's all over Ukraine?

Our military continues to defend Kyiv. At night, explosions and machine gun fire were heard in various parts of the capital, in the morning, the Russians fired on residential neighbourhoods, an enemy shell hit a 25-storey building, and there were casualties. Residents were urged to stay in shelters, as well as follow the rules of conduct during the shelling.

During the attack on Kharkiv, the Russians used cluster bombs with the Petal mines banned by the Geneva Convention.

Chernihiv also continued to defend itself, where the city was shelled from "Grad". The shelling of at least 15 residential buildings, as well as kindergartens and gas stations, was known. The situation was also difficult in Sumy.

Heavy fighting continued in southern Ukraine.

Losses of the Russian occupiers

During the day, Russian troops lost at least 11 helicopters of various types, three Su-30 SM fighters, two Su-25 attack aircraft and another military transport IL-76 MD with an occupant landing.

The Su-24M front-line bomber smashed a column of 20 units of military equipment in one fell swoop.

As of the morning of February 26, the Ukrainian military had killed more than 3,500 Russians defending their territory. More than 200 enemies were taken prisoner.

At the Beresteiska metro station in Kyiv, our military destroyed an enemy column, including two cars, two trucks and a tank.

Losses of the Ukrainian Armed Forces and civilians

A few more statistics:

According to the Minister of Health, during the two days of the war, the Russians have killed 198 civilians, including 3 children. We also have 1,115 wounded civilians, including 33 children. But I'm sure that later those numbers would be recalculated and would be bigger...

In Kyiv, two people were killed and six were seriously injured in the shelling of a high-rise building. While checking the documents, unknown people killed a policeman, after which they fled in a car.

In Kyiv region, four people were injured and a child died due to the collapse of a bridge on the Kyiv-Kovel-Yagodyn highway. In the village of Borodyanka, a shell hit a residential building, killing three people.

Near Kherson, the occupiers lined up an ambulance carrying the wounded. The driver and the patient were killed; the paramedic was wounded. I've seen those photos... That's awful, and it's against any humanitarian or war rules to kill medics...

In Donetsk region, the occupiers fired on peaceful settlements, killing at least 19 civilians.

Day 3 gathered even more people in different countries. Britain, Georgia, USA, France, Germany, Italy... I can't name the country that do not know about the war, except most Russians...

One girl contacted my friend on Instagram with a text: "You know what? Why does no-one talk about the thing that Spotify is blocked in Russia? Or that I'll not be able to fly to Paris? By the way I really wanted to go to Paris this month. Why don't you post about this? Is it important only that people are dying in Ukraine? It's hypocrisy.

I was like: "Really??? Is it only the thing you worry about?? People are dying from your President. Not only Ukrainians, but Russian soldiers too. It's hypocrisy to think just about yourself and your wishes today."

One more case. One famous Russian blogger posted." Why am I seeing just the same videos with bombs? Explosions or fire? Why don't you see many people? It's me, this is my flat"

And lots of comments to that post – "like are you filming when someone tries to kill you??"

Actually, later one of my friends Nikita were recording a video of how he was helping everyone and he was hit by some explosion.

Really, it seems like many Russian people live in another reality or dimension.

But, luckily not all of them. And I've seen lots of rallies to support Ukraine in big cities like Moscow or St Petersburg. But people are afraid. They are caught by the police and imprisoned, often beaten. Even children.

I've read a story about one old woman like 80+ y.o and she was ready to be arrested but went to this place of the meeting to support Ukraine. But she was a World War II veteran. When Police asked her - who encouraged you to do this? She answered- I would do it by myself alone, if no-one would do the same. Cause it's about our brotherly people. And we were against Hitler together... And really, for many years we celebrated the 9th of May together, and now all this against Ukraine...

And that video where a really old man without a leg with dozens of medals on his chest after the World War II ... He talked to the Russian police officer and he was crying and asking him: "Tell me, for what have I lost my leg? I had a huge hole in my stomach... what was all of this for??? It's a real World War 3" He cried ...

They can't understand this war, as well as Ukrainians can't understand it. The same as those young men in tanks who were sent by Putler to die for his money or his obsessive idea to seize Ukraine...

Dialogues or Russian soldiers

Dialogue of Russian soldier and his mom:

- Alexey, why have you not answered our messages for such a long time?
- Mom, I'm not on training any more, not in Crimea.
- But where???? Dad is asking if we can send you some parcel.
- What parcel? I just wanna die now.
- What? What happened?

- Mom, I'm in Ukraine. There is a real war here… I'm scared. we kill everyone, even peaceful ones. All people in a row. We were told they would greet us, but they threw themselves under our vehicles and did not let us pass. They call us fascists. Mom, it is very hard for me.

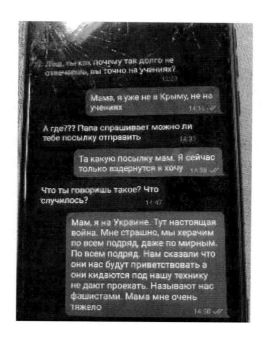

One more dialogue of a Russian soldier and his girl:

- I'm captured now. We came here, it turns out, but they deceived us that we came to defend, and on the contrary, we came to kill civilians, children …

- Vania, what are you talking about??? Vania…what are you talking about?

- Call the wife of Yuri Omelyanenko, tell them to call the hotline and find out how to pick up the bodies ..

- What bodies?

- Their bodies…

- Will they let you go home?

- I don't know, I hope..

- I really want to hug you

- Vania, you will definitely hug

- I love you so much

- We love you too

- F*ck this army. You come home and quit this army…

Also, on this day in Kyiv, an old man was crushed by a tank. He was just driving his car somewhere .... I don't know really how, but he survived. Some passers-by pulled him out of the tank and called an ambulance. In Ukraine we say "born in a shirt". It's when a person was lucky to survive.

Fourth Day of the War

February 27, 2022

The fourth day of the war began with man-made disasters:

Russian troops blew up a gas pipeline in the Kharkiv region, burning an oil depot near Vasylkiv (the one is that is close to the location of the family of my close friend).

What was that day?

A missile strike was fired from a military unit near Vladimir in Belarus. Iskander missiles from Belarus were also launched in

Zhytomyr. Another missile fired at Kyiv was successfully shot down by our military.

The Ukrainian military is defending Kyiv and preventing the enemy from breaking into the capital. During the shelling of Bucha, near Kyiv, one of the rockets hit a nine storey residential building.

The situation is also tense in Chernihiv, where on February 27 Russians aimed at the city council, children's and adult dentistry, administrative buildings and high-rise residential buildings were affected.

Meanwhile, in Kryukivtsi, Chernihiv Oblast, police and civilians stopped Russian tanks without firing a single shot. They simply blocked an entrance by themselves to their village. Brave people! Proud of you!

There were explosions in Kherson and Kharkiv. In particular, enemy vehicles were able to break into Kharkiv. In Kyiv groups of 5-10 Russians were being taken prisoner by the Ukrainian military, throwing equipment in the middle of the road.

Near Kyiv, the Ukrainian military destroyed a Russian convoy of more than 100 units of armored vehicles. A column of the elite 141st Motorized Regiment of the Chechen Rosguard was also defeated near Gostomel and its commander, Magomed Tushayev, was killed. Chechen Rosguard - can you imagine???

In Kharkiv, the Ukrainian military destroyed a column of Russian Tigers.

The shelling continued in Kyiv! And they really tried to realise a plan to get Kyiv and Kharkiv. But we will resist!

Up until the 4th day, the Ukrainian military had destroyed more than 700 armored combat vehicles, 150 tanks, 27 aircraft, 26 helicopters, 50 guns, 30 cars, 60 tanks, "ridges", as well as more than 4.5 thousand Russians.

Important statements

All EU countries supported Russia's disconnection from SWIFT. Russia's disconnection from SWIFT will limit its access to global financial markets. This will hit the country's economy. Until now, Hungary and Germany have refrained from their official position on additional sanctions against Russia.

What is SWIFT?

SWIFT is a mechanism for transferring data and making payments between banks all over the world. Payment orders are sent securely using this method by more than 11,000 financial institutions in over 200 countries and territories. Every day, the system handles billions of dollars in transactions. It is the world's most major financial system, governed by the central banks of Europe, the United States, Canada, and Japan.

What consequences will Russia feel after the shutdown?

Because it would restrict Russia's access to global financial markets, cutting it off from the network will pose major economic consequences.

As a result of the embargo, it will be more difficult for Russian businesses and individuals to import items or obtain payment for commodities exported. The oil and gas industry will be the worst damaged. It will also hinder Russian citizens' capacity to invest or borrow overseas.

Other methods of transferring cash and processing payments in Russia, such as using banks that have not been sanctioned, are also available. As far as transaction volume and security go, no other technique can match SWIFT's.

Germany has announced the provision of anti-tank weapons and Stingers to Ukraine. The German federal government, which has been opposed to arms supplies to Ukraine for weeks, has approved a decision to provide the Armed Forces with 1,000 anti-tank weapons and 500 Stinger anti-aircraft missiles.

Turkey has closed the passage to the Black Sea for Russian warships. According to President Zelensky, it will also provide military and humanitarian assistance to Ukraine, but he did not specify what it is about.

Some other positive information about that day and how ordinary people all over the world support Ukraine:

Georgians refused to refuel Russian ships and offered them to use paddles.

The dialogue was like:

- You look like Russian. Are you from Russia?

- Yes, from Russia.

- Okay, the crew from Russia, right? Guys, we refuse to supply your steamer.

- Who is talking to us?

- The capitan mate from Georgia is talking to you and we will not supply your steamer. Russian warship, go fuck yourself. (He repeated the legendary phrase in Russian, that the heroes from Zmiinyi Island answered to occupiers).

- Dear, no politics, please. We're running out of fuel.

- Well, if you run out of fuel, you can use the oars. Glory to the heroes! (in Ukrainian)

This video has been seen by every Ukrainian and we consider it a gesture of humanity from our Georgian friends. And that money is not more important than people!

In Ukraine, no-one will stop. In the village of Lyubimovka in the Kherson region, gypsies on a tractor stole a tank from the Russians.

What was important that day that Ukrainians realised that Russian navigation worked really bad in Ukraine, cause they started to ask civilians where to go. From that moment it became one more of our advantages.

In one village, an old man "helped" Russians to cut the road and they got stuck with their equipment in the swamp. People started to tell them a wrong way.

From that moment, people started to remove or change road signs. They changed them to "go back to Russia" or towards "go f*ck yourself".

Once Russian soldier asked a village woman the right way. And she answered him the wrong one, but also she gave him some sunflower seeds (it's popular in Ukraine and Russia to eat them) . She told him "Put them in your pocket, maybe when you die at least you'll have some fertilizer in your pocket".

Fifth Day of the War

February 27, 2022

People all over the world started to help Ukraine by sending some humanitarian aid, money (Ukrainian national bank opened a special account to save the lives of Ukrainians - named 'Savelife'), even International soldiers started to arrive to Ukraine to help us.

A lot of refugees are trying to get to the borders. Basically, it is women and children. Men cannot leave the country.

But not everyone could be a soldier of the "National Defence". Many men wanted to take up arms and defend the country, but there were some limits. So, they helped as they could with preparing Molotov cocktails or protecting their families, or sometimes gathering and block roads to Russian troops.

The attack of Russian troops on Ukrainian cities went wrong according to Vladimir Putin's plan: Ukrainians hold the defence and destroy the enemy. However, the Russians are not only at war with the military, but are also shooting civilians… (Women and children die from enemy bullets. For example, in Berdyansk, Russians shot a man for refusing to give away a mobile phone, and in Mariupol, the enemy killed a six-year-old girl. A little girl, just 6 y.o. How? And they said they came to protect us. From whom????

This day was important for Ukraine because we applied to join the EU.

Joining the EU. What does it mean for Ukraine?

In a morning video address on February 28, President Volodymyr Zelensky stated that Ukraine had appealed to the EU for Ukraine's immediate accession under a new special procedure.

And the first ceasefire talks between Ukrainian and Russian delegations took place.

The first talks between the Ukrainian and Russian delegations on ending the war in Ukraine. The parties have not yet agreed on a ceasefire. That was expected, cause when Russia tried to get DNR and LNR, it wasn't the only one meeting.

But people really expected the war would over soon. A lot of sanctions were applied to Russia and the Russian economy will very soon have a default.

Ukraine announced promises to give the Russian military 5 million Rubles after the capture.

For the first time in history, Switzerland had violated its neutrality and was imposing sanctions on Russia. Five Russian oligarchs close to Vladimir Putin have been banned from entering Switzerland.

Officially, in order to join the European Union, any European country could apply for membership in the Council of the EU. The Council of the European Union is currently chaired by France, which has repeatedly declared its support for Ukraine.

The Council must then decide to refer it to the European Commission for an application, which may be considered for several months under the standard procedure.

A new special procedure for Ukraine's accession to the EU had been proposed by Slovak Prime Minister Eduard Heger.

"They fight for themselves, they fight for us — they fight for freedom," Eduard Heger said in an interview with Politico on February 27.

At the same time, Eduard Heger did not specify what the procedure for Ukraine's simplified accession to the EU should look like. However, he noted that this procedure should provide assistance to Ukraine for post-war reconstruction.

In the previous day, the Russian occupiers fired six missiles (up to 30 missiles) and four air strikes, mostly from Belarus. Since the beginning of the open aggression, the enemy has used about 180 Iskander cruise and operational-tactical missiles.

Kharkiv is being shelled from the "Grad", dozens of civilians are dying because of the Russian army. Due to the tense situation, Kharkiv region became the first in Ukraine to establish a curfew during the day: from 16:00 to 06:00.

The situation in Sumy was also difficult, the mayor urges locals to be ready for street fights. In Okhtyrka, the Russians blew up an oil depot during an attack on the city. The Russian military attacked the town of Brovary near Kyiv from the air, injuring six people.

Chernihiv continued to defend the city, and Russian troops have been attacking the homes of civilians from the air. In the morning, a rocket hit a residential building in the centre of Chernihiv, about 15 residential buildings in the city had already been shelled.

Losses of the Russian occupiers

During the four days of the Russian-Ukrainian war, about 5,300 Russian servicemen have been killed. Armed Forces of

Ukraine Destroyed Russian Base of 96 Tanks and 20 Grads in Sumy Region

In total, Ukrainians shot down 29 enemy planes, 29 helicopters, destroyed 191 tanks, 816 armoured combat vehicles, 74 guns, one beech SAM, 21 Grad, 291 cars, destroyed 60 tanks, 3 OTP UAVs, 2 ships, 5 air defence equipment.

Losses of the Ukrainian Armed Forces and civilians

The enemy continues to attack Kharkiv, the city is being shelled en masse from the "Grad". The mayor of Kharkiv said that during the day in the city 9 people have been killed, 37 injured, including three children. The Russians killed four people who came out of the bomb shelter to collect water. A family of five (three children) also have been burned alive in a car. But, I'm sure that the numbers will be higher when they count it when the war is over. Constantly I see the information that someone is looking for his/her friends or relatives...

Since yesterday, the Berdyansk district in the Zaporizhya region is being occupied by Russians. At least two people were injured during the capture of the city: one was killed and another was wounded. The regional state administration reports that in Berdyansk itself, Russians shot a civilian for refusing to return his mobile phone.

A 6-year-old girl died in the port of Mariupol from Russian shelling.

During the war, Putin, so far, has killed more than 350 civilians and wounded 1,684 others. In addition, killing nine police officers and wounded 27.

The great thing in Ukraine has been that people became one nation, unity, solidarity - where everyone wants peace in their own country.

Everyone has been helping in a way they can. Ukrainian IT experts have created ab anonymous group that has dozens of hackers and they have been trying to help Russians to understand what's going on.

As a result, on Russian TV, instead of Russian news they have started to show Ukrainian songs. One day later they shown them a freshly made war video with a poem by the famous singer Monatik.

People in Ukraine have created lots of channels to help each other. With money transferring, food, supporting moms, there has been a problem with the internet and my friends have created a telegram channel with fairy tales, that could be easily downloaded when people had internet and then listened when they were offline.

Also, I should say that it's an info war. A lot of fake news has started to appear, like that some cities surrendered to the occupier. But, people have reacted fast and informed each other ASAP about all fake news.

Ukrainians have been very attentive regarding the information, cause often their lives depend on how fast they could get information. Information about the situation in Ukraine was on the Instagram accounts of my every Ukrainian friend, if they could post and were it is safe of course... Sometimes, it was about looking for friends, relatives, sometimes, people needed help with food, sometimes about bombs and shelling, sometimes looking for new parents for the children whose parents had died. But, most often I think it was about trying to get out of the city and go to the western part of Ukraine or abroad, a safer place. Everyone just want to lives... but also to live in FREEDOM! Without censorship and dictatorship.

People have started to add war pictures in Russia in Google Maps. So, maybe now if you want to find some restaurant in Russia, you'll see the last comments with tanks, explosions or soldiers who hase sadly died instead of nice photos of the meals.

Some helpful apps have been invented, like an app to inform about the danger, a kind of a siren. In some cities for some reason, sirens haven't worked and thus, church bells also could be used like sirens. New websites have been created to help each other where you can ask for help or become a volunteer and help others…

I think that people have actively developed the stage of accepting the situation and mass helping each other. *"Разом нас багато, нас не подолати"*. "All together there are many of us, we will not be defeated".

What's in Russia?

Most people have just started to understand that there is a war in Ukraine. Russian war. And their sons are dying here. Their TV simply zombies people and does not let them understand that there are others outside their country.

They are less and less afraid to go to rallies. Yes, people are beaten by the police. Yes, old people and children are imprisoned for peaceful rallies. But, they began to realise that at the same time, other civilians were being killed … cities are being destroyed by Russian soldiers.

The Ruble exchange rate has begun to grow.

A huge part of the sky has been closed for them. People who were returning home from different countries have had delays because planes were looking for alternative ways. But honestly maybe it would be better for them to not return.

They can't use Apple pay, so they have started to have problems with payments in the underground, supermarkets.

A lot of entertainments like Netflix, Spotify closed access to Russia.

Many companies have decided to close or implement some limits in Russia. On day 7, more than 90 international companies have been involved and taken actions against this hostile country.

Russians have started to realise that their life is changing not for the better. Maybe they used internet to research what was going on and what was the reason.

But people have got some limits and even those changes have forced them to re-think.

Even here, Ukrainians have come up with a joke, that Porn Hub have also left Russia.

But, actually Onlyfans.com did. They have made it impossible for Russian users to get some money from this platform.

Many celebrities support Ukraine, but not all of them. It seems to me that they were so dependent on Putin and were so afraid of him that it has prevented them from recognising the war. But most of their Instagram accounts have been blocked by Ukrainians for hate speeches or Russian propaganda.

Conclusions

These 5 days of the war represent a gigantic struggle for Ukrainians. Many people have been killed, many homes have been destroyed. The infrastructure of many cities are ruined. The goal of Russia is to capture large cities like Kyiv, Kharkov, and they believe that then Ukraine will surrender. But no...

We realized that our strength is our unity. We've realized that the Russian soldiers were lied to and they do not understand that they are going to seize foreign territory and they will be rebuffed here.

Russia did not expect such support from the European Union and other countries to Ukraine, a small country, but as it has turned out one with a big heart and patriotism. A lot of things have so far been accomplished to ensure that Ukraine will survive. And we will resist!

Ukrainians remain people, united people. They just want to live on their territory, peacefully doing their own business and protecting their families...

Made in United States
North Haven, CT
22 April 2022

18463133R00033